Talk & Talkers

In my opinion, the most fruitful and natural play of the mind is conversation. I find it sweeter than any action in life.

Montaigne, "On the Art of Conversation"

Copyright © 1989 Jana Stone and Ozubko Design

Photograph selections copyright © 1989 Thom Sempere

Seattle Post Intelligencer Collection, Museum of History and Industry, Page 8, Page 25; Wilcox Collection, Museum of History and Industry, Page 14; Museum of History and Industry Collection, Page 20; Seattle, Washington.

Special Collections Division, University of Washington Libraries, Seattle; Cover Photograph: UW Neg No. 10015; Page 11: UW Neg No. 10228; Page 12: UW Neg No. 9989; Page 17: UW Neg No. 10014; Page 19: UW Neg No. 10260; Page 22: UW Neg No. 9806.

Published in 1989 by
Stewart, Tabori & Chang, Inc.
740 Broadway, New York, New York 10003

All rights reserved. No part of the contents of this book may be reproduced by any means without the written permission of the publisher.

ISBN: 1-55670-114-4

Printed in Italy

EXCERPTS FROM THE ESSAY

Talk & Talkers

ROBERT LOUIS
Stevenson

Photographs Researched by Thom Sempere

STEWART, TABORI & CHANG   NEW YORK

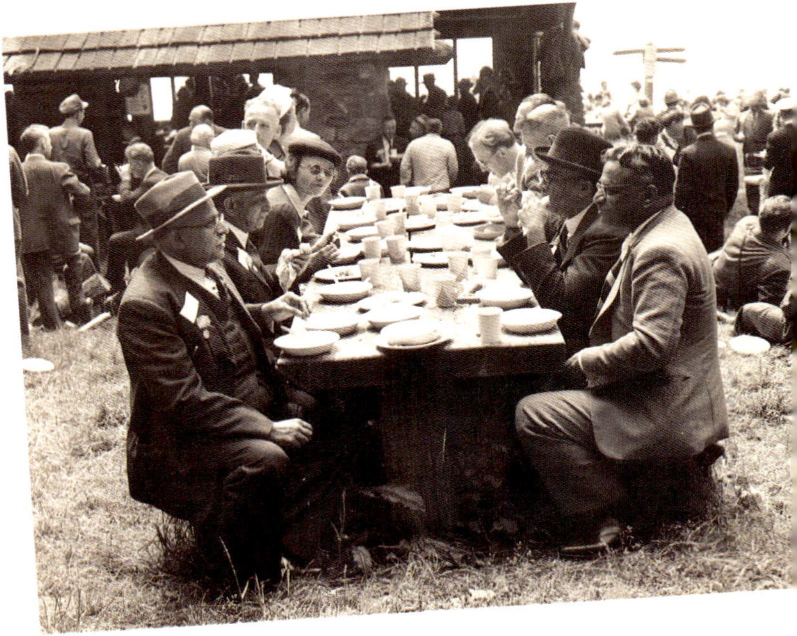

Talk & Talkers

There can be no fairer ambition than to excel in talk; to be affable, gay, ready, clear and welcome; to have a fact, a thought, or an illustration, pat to every subject; and not only to cheer the flight of time among our intimates, but to bear our part in that great international congress, always sitting....No measure comes before Parliament but it has been long ago prepared by the grand jury of the talkers; no book is written that has not been largely composed by their assistance. Literature in many of its branches is no other than the shadow of good talk; but the imitation falls far short of the original in life, freedom and effect.

Stevenson

Talk & Talkers

Talk is fluid, tentative, continually "in further search and progress"; while written words remain fixed, become idols even to the writer, found wooden dogmatisms, and preserve files of obvious error in the amber of truth. Last and chief, while literature... can only deal with a fraction of the life of man, talk goes fancy free and may call a spade a spade.

venson

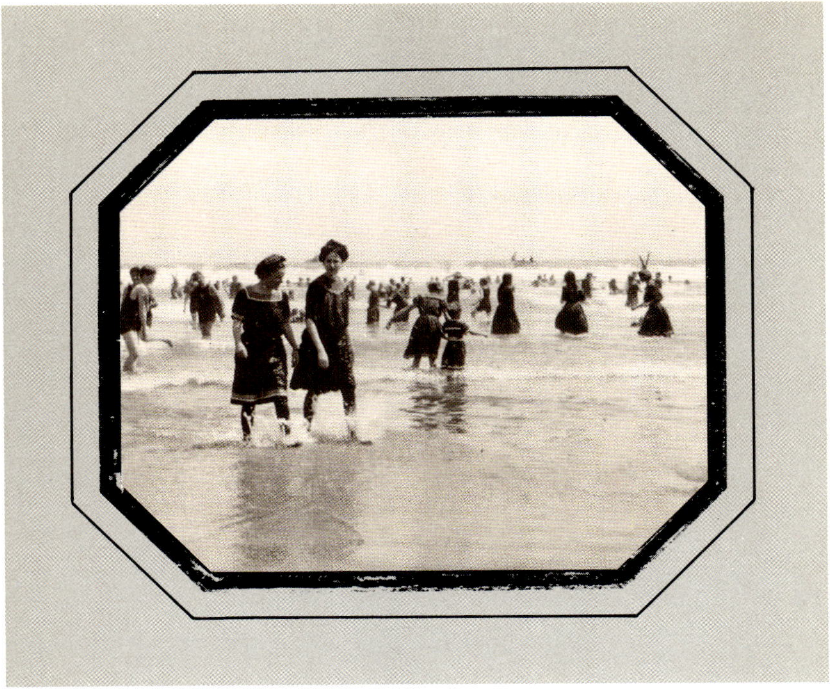

Talk & Talkers

It is in talk alone that we can learn our period and ourselves. In short, the first duty of a man is to speak; that is his chief business in this world; and talk, which is the harmonious speech of two or more, is by far the most accessible of pleasures. It costs nothing in money; it is all profit; it completes our education, founds and fosters our friendships, and can be enjoyed at any age and in almost any state of health.

. . . .

Stevenson

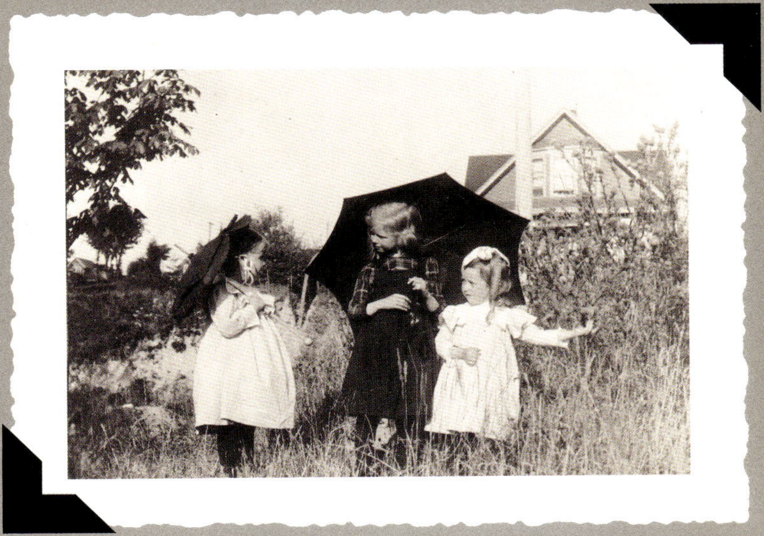

14

Talk & Talkers

Talk is, indeed, both the scene and instrument of friendship. It is in talk alone that the friends can measure strength, and enjoy that amicable counter-assertion of personality which is the gauge of relations and the sport of life.

Stevenson

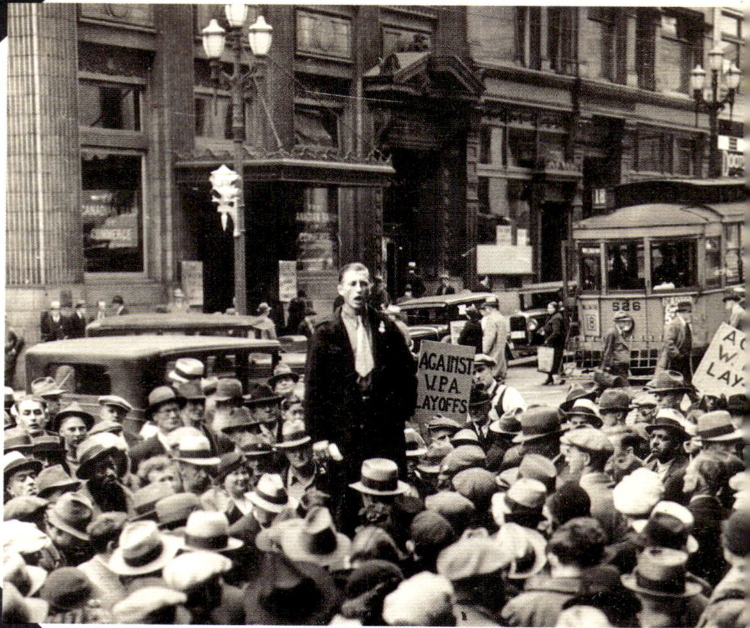
AGAINST
W.P.A.
LAYOFFS
526

Talk & Talkers

All natural talk is a festival of ostentation; and by the laws of the game each accepts and fans the vanity of the other. It is from that reason that we venture to lay ourselves so open, that we dare to be so warmly eloquent, and that we swell in each other's eyes to such a vast proportion. For talkers, once launched, begin to overflow the limits of their ordinary selves, tower up to the height of their secret pretentions, and give themselves out for heroes, brave, pious, musical and wise, that in their most shining moments they aspire to be.

Stevenson

Talk & Talkers

The genuine artist follows the stream of conversation as an angler follows the windings of a brook, not dallying where he fails to "kill." He trusts implicitly to hazard; and he is rewarded by continual variety, continual pleasure, and those changing prospects of the truth that are the best education. There is nothing in a subject, so called, that we should regard it as an idol, or follow it beyond the promptings of desire. Indeed, there are few subjects; and so far as they are truly talkable, more than half of them may be reduced to three: that I am I, that you are you, and that there are other people dimly understand to be not quite the same as either.

. . . .

Stevenson

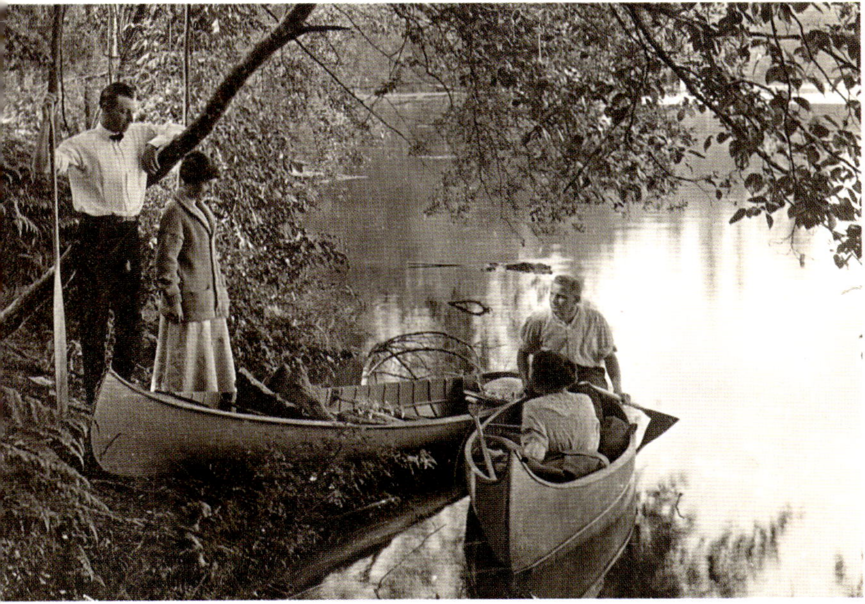

Talk & Talkers

Natural talk, like ploughing, should turn up a large surface of life, rather than dig mines into geological strata. Masses of experience, anecdote, incident, crosslights, quotation, historical instances, the whole flotsam and jetsam of two minds forced in and in upon the matter in hand from every point of the compass, and from every degree of mental elevation and abasement—these are the material with which talk is fortified, the food on which the talkers thrive. Such argument as is proper to the exercise should still be brief and seizing. Talk should proceed by instances; by the apposite not the expository. It should keep close along the lines of humanity, near the bosoms and businesses of men, at the level where history, fiction and experience intersect and illuminate each other. I am I, and You are You, with all my heart; but conceive how these lean propositions change and brighten when, instead of words, the actual you and I sit cheek by jowl, the spirit housed in the live body, and the very clothes uttering voices to corroborate the story in the face.

. . . .

Stevenson

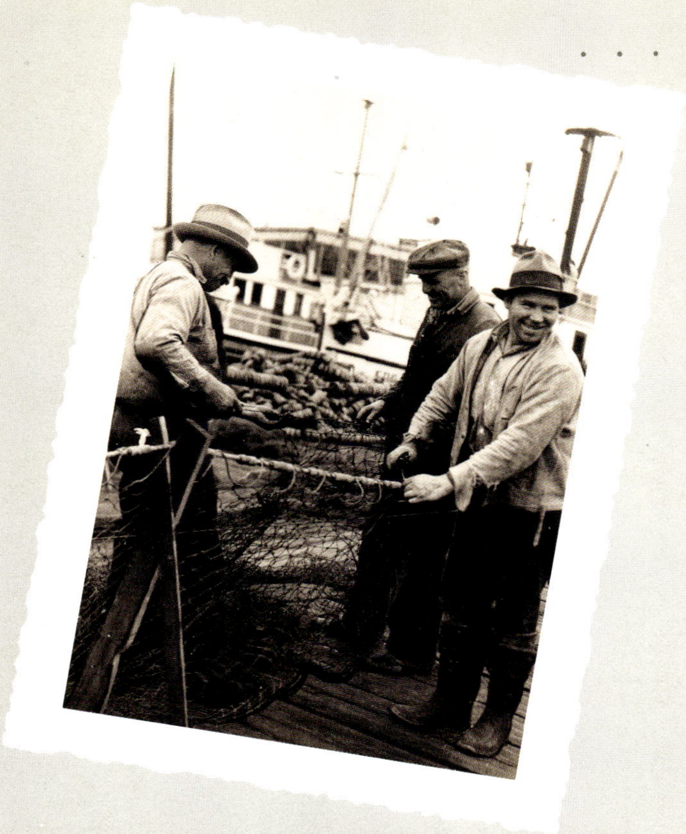

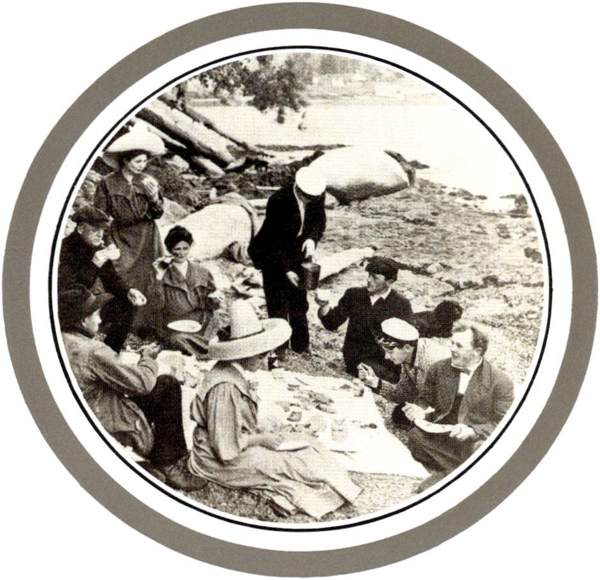

Talk & Talkers

There is a certain attitude, combative at once and deferential, eager to fight yet most adverse to quarrel, which marks out at once the talkable man. It is not eloquence, not fairness, not obstinancy, but a certain proportion of all these that I love to encounter in my amicable adversaries. They must not be pontiffs holding doctrine, but huntsmen questing after elements of truth. Neither must they be boys to be instructed, but fellow-teachers with whom I may wrangle and agree on equal terms. We must reach some solution, some shadow of consent; for without that, eager talk becomes torture. But we do not wish to reach it cheaply, or quickly, or without the tussle and effort wherein pleasure lies.

. . . .

Stevenson

Talk & Talkers

Most of us, by the Protean quality of
man, can talk to some degree with
all; but the true talk, that strikes out
all the slumbering best of us, comes
only with the peculiar brethren of
our spirits, is founded as deep as
love in the constitution of our being,
and is a thing to relish with all our
energy, while yet we have it, and to
be grateful for for ever.

Stevenson

Robert Louis Stevenson

ROBERT LOUIS STEVENSON

1 8 5 0 - 1 8 9 4

Scottish novelist and essayist

Robert Louis Stevenson is best known for those beloved classics **Kidnapped, Treasure Island,** and **Dr. Jekyll and Mr. Hyde.** Yet in his lifetime, Stevenson was as widely known as an essayist as for these grand tales of romance and adventure. Contributing to a variety of periodicals that included **MacMillan's, Scribner's,** and Leslie Stephen's **Cornhill Magazine,** Stevenson produced an eclectic body of short works. Whether literary criticism, biographical study, travel reporting, or personal essay, his writing was marked by a warm humanity and delightful humor that managed to combine a moral sense with an aesthetic sensibility. Nowhere was this better demonstrated than in his personal essays as he wittily examined idleness in "An Apology for Idlers," courtship in "On Falling in Love," the imagination in "The Lantern-Bearers," or the art of conversation in "Talk and Talkers." Published in 1881, "Talk and Talkers" was a quintessential Stevenson essay, celebrating the friendship and community that could only be realized through the spoken word.

Though plagued by ill health all of his life, Stevenson traveled widely—often in search of healthier climates—through Europe, America, and the South Seas. He made his final home in Samoa, where he died at the age of 44 and lies buried atop Mount Vaea.

COLOPHON

Photo Research

Thom Sempere
Seattle, Washington

Process

Images selected from various archives
and private collections. New prints
made from original photos and hand-toned

Typeface

Sabon and Clarendon

Typesetting

Western Type
Seattle, Washington

Separations, Printing, and Binding

Arnoldo Mondadori Editore S.p.A.
Verona, Italy

Stock

170gsm Gardamatte

Design

Ozubko Design

Series Editor

Jana Stone